DON'T CROSS THAT CREEK: GO AND ASK YOUR FATHER

DON'T CROSS THAT CREEK: GO AND ASK YOUR FATHER

KENNETH R. DAVIS

Library of Congress Control Number: 2023912074

ISBN:	Hardcover	979-8-3694-0222-1
	Softcover	979-8-3694-0221-4
	eBook	979-8-3694-0220-7

Print information available on the last page.

Rev. date: 07/13/2023

To order additional copies of this book, contact:
Xlibris
844-714-8691
www.Xlibris.com
Orders@Xlibris.com
852999

Dedication

Prayer is a spiritual & personal form of hope....in a very sincere way or "asking". Never stop your daily affirmations of prayer....prayer is our most potent medicine....but positive action is the cure.

I dedicate this book to my parents, my children, my siblings, and the remainder of my entire family tree. I love you and please continue to protect your freedom(s).

Kendrick, Kenya, Kendell, Alexis, and Noah....I love you! Protect your freedom(s), continue to chase your dreams, and no person on earth can stop you from reaching your milestones & dreams. I surround you with this comfort which is one of my favorite original phrases: I believe in you; I trust you; I love you!

Purpose

I wrote this book specifically for my kids and to unlock the voices & thoughts of my parents & grandparents. To my children: You are why I write! You will never have to ask "the world" to allow you to be successful....success is already part of your DNA. You will never have to ask permission to be smart, great, handsome, beautiful, likeable, intelligent, accepted, etc. I stand on the shoulders of giants...like my parents. Thus, I definitely give thanks to my parents for teaching me the value of speaking up & out. My children, your father have already given you the valuable gifts and traits that you will need to continue to be great! Now, by all means, go and continue to be great! Hallelujah & God bless Your World! You own the World! You can do anything & everything! I love you more!!!

Preface

Hello World! Hello America! I surmise that this nation's biggest sin is slavery! Secondly, I also assert that this racist-fake nation, that we call America, feeds off its modern-day practices of at least 7 types of racism: representational, ideological, discursive, interactional, institutional, structural, & systemic. Yet, as we continue to strategically and successfully maneuver through every turn, we have been somewhat fooled to think that freedom is something that we have to ask for.... or conquer. Nevertheless, we should never forget that "real freedom" is the ability to express your thoughts orally or otherwise. Actually, simply put, your only real freedom, physically or emotionally, is to speak your truth! Ergo, therefore, freedom is not found in a written document; it also does not represent something that someone gives to you either. Freedom is a birthright; freedom belongs to you from a spiritual & ethical sense...you are born into freedom. Freedom is innately yours & cannot ever be denied or taken away!

Furthermore, one should speak his or her truth whether it fills the room or clears the room. Speak and celebrate your truth! Will your truth sometimes bring about unintended consequences? Absolutely! Yet, you are free! You are free on the inside! You are the epitome of freedom! This is just one example of what this racist country and evil world continue to exploit....yet, you are free! In the meantime, grab your freedom and enjoy some of my original inspirations, expressions, and general thoughts. Finally, if by chance you disagree with a word or two....it's okay. Whether you are Black, White, Indigenous, Hispanic, Asian, or any other race....it's okay to disagree with a few of my expressions. Yet, after you disagree, just move forward with your new-found enthusiasm....and write your own book. Enjoy the inspirations!

I love you and you know that God loves you too....I love you!

While thanking God for all the things that you do have....don't forget to also give God thanks for blocking or denying some of the things that you "thought" you should have received along the way. He was looking out for you....for all of us....even when you cannot see 10, 20, 30, years ahead of our own lives

After God....love yourself more than any other "selves". Why? It's hard loving someone else if you do not love yourself first. We all have our days of "hills & valleys"....just do not stop loving you....even when you feel "down in the valley"

I have but one true dream left on this earth: to be my sons & daughters first hero & their first real love. All of my other subsequent dreams....are built upon that very foundation

When life appears very depressing or stressful....just continue. Continue to love yourself, continue to stay strong, continue your mission, and continue to know that I love you very much!

Excellence is....Black Excellence; Excellence is You

As a Black man or woman, the world will often refer to you as an inanimate object....but just know that when I created & made you... you are the «positive subject and never a negative object». I made you that way: positively essential!!!

The Great Awakening is all about believing in something greater than you. It is also never allowing evil folks "to pull the wool over your eyes" either. Therefore, the Great Awakening equals being awaken & staying woke. Stay woke my brother....stay woke my sister! Stay Woke!!

Don't allow the world to control, dismiss, misrepresent, use, or misuse your unique authenticity; your authenticity belongs solely to you; just you and not your parents, family, friends, teachers, mentors, pastors, etc. Stay true to yourself and your truths! Stay authentic my sons & daughters!

Celebrate your victories regardless of how big or small the victories may be; all of your victories are hugely important

If you want to reach and grab your future, then you will have to let go of anything in your past.... (especially the negatives of your past)

Know that I have already validated you for everything you need in life. Yet, the human nature portion of us....often attempts to seek even more validation from other sources. When....or if you determine that you need to be validated....never look backwards to any past person, organization, or past relationship for that validation. For example, your old friends, your childhood church, your old team, your old group of friends, or your high school, your old classmates, your last jobs, your last projects or ventures, and etc....cannot validate you. Validation comes from your dad or father. Yet, just in case more validation is wanted....you will quickly realize that validation only lies ahead of you....never behind you. You....validate you! Besides, you are already validated....with Dad's stamp of approval. I stamped you with my "approval of excellence"!

Focus your energies more on being spiritual (belief in the one & only God)....and way, way less focus on being religious (fakers who make up a set of cult-like beliefs & follow anything)

These quick troubles....better known as the "Easy 7 Troubles".... could easily prevent you from advancement, growth, promotion, positive fame, or glamour: inadequate sleep, alcohol, drugs, law trouble, improper gun use, inappropriate conduct, and finally, being with a woman who you know as well as being with a woman who you do not know. Those are the daily troubles....be safe & be careful....and always know danger when you encounter it

You have the necessary food that will feed the world....yet every corner of the world has not being thoroughly introduced to your talent & knowledge to feed it's people; you will feed the world. You will continue to feed the world via your knowledge, talents, caring spirit, intelligence, skills, abilities, leadership, business ownership, and plenty of other categories as well. Stay tuned....my kids will shake up the world! I can't wait to see or hear what you do next!

True Manhood: quickly closes all situations & thoroughly satisfied with never looking for closure in any situation; never looking to receive answers but gives answers; never sacrifice his inner peace for anybody or anything

True Womanhood: follows her man....supports her man....and waits to be told by her man....on what she can and cannot do. She never tries to emasculate her man. That's the essence of being a woman

The one thing that most adults do not verbally tell teenagers & young adults: you have to quickly learn how to "parent yourself". Simply put....you have to constantly & consistently make yourself do those things that you do not want to do. Does it sucks? Yes....it does, but it's very necessary on the road towards "growth & development" (that full maturation process)

You stand on the shoulders of "Giants"....such as your Dad, Parents, Grandparents, & Great Grandparents. Think about that blessing often....because there is no way that we could have "made it" without the sacrifices of these elite giants & warriors. This is why you are already a giant & a warrior! Stay mindful....stay blessed!

My 4 nuggets of Wisdom and/or Virtue: 1) surround yourself with folks who love you more than you love them, 2) you do not have to work like slaves to be successful....just work smarter than the other people; 3) say "I love you" to yourself & to someone else everyday (say it to children, parents, friends, strangers, etc.); 4) facing enemy-type of trouble: run (away or toward the problem), hide (stay silent for a short time), or fight (out think your opponent by coming up with a solution, or as a last resort....be physical only in self defense.... or when appropriate). Remember that the best "physical fight"....is to smartly & strongly walk away from the perceived enemy....if you can. Finally, number 5)....once you identify which heavenly star that you want to climb....go and climb it. Before you climb it....just realize that there will always be another star left to be climbed....and the next one is at a different elevation than the last one. Keep going.... your stars are plentiful....just do not forget to properly rest....every day....along the journey!

It's okay to be nice to folks, it's okay to do favors for folks, it's okay to make sacrifices for folks....but you owe nobody your soul or your life....nobody. Your life belongs to you....and you only!

Sometimes....our greatest strength is to "remain silent"....show the enemy your silence when nothing else appears to make sense. At other times, that same enemy sometimes need to be shown the lion.... so that he can appreciate the true lamb that you truly are. The most difficult piece of this puzzle is this: you have nothing to prove to anyone....at any time. Therefore, you can always find comfort in.... "walking away" from danger....to include any heated debates. Find your comfort zone, your angle, your approach, & your very own debate/leadership style. Again, I already know how great you are.... no one else matters

Speak your true feelings, ideas, suggestions, & etc....with your chest; you may feel bad for a second or even for a few days....or even a few months....but that feeling will get better with the passage of time (this bitter-sweet feeling is just confirmation that you are still human.... capable of showing real emotions)

Keep your positive & negative emotions somewhat balanced.... because negative people will use your positive or negative emotions against you at the worst moments...so be very careful who you display your true emotions to. Every person does not have to know everything that you are thinking and feeling. Find that one person or just a couple of close friends to share those personal details with at various times

In God we trust, and everybody else must sign (trust yourself & nobody else....or at a minimal....depending on the subject....trust other people very, very, very little....but strongly verify). In all things....trust but verify!

A man does not get the luxury of choosing his passion....instead, his real passion chooses him. My children....I am passionate about you....because you chose me & I honor your choice. You are my real passion! In addition to investing in humankind, find your passion.... then become an expert at it. Here's another secret: I chose you too!

Equality, justice, and freedom should feel uncomfortable but it should not ever feel like torture or punishment to the opposite race of people. If one feels like it is torture or punishment....then he or she is very much a racist ...or at the very least....she or he is not anti-racist

For those races of people who are not "of color"....show me one "anti-racist" thing that you did this week? Last week? Last month? If you can not show me such an action....then you are most likely a racist! The formula is simple....very simple indeed....debate closed

Here is one thing that anti-racist people could do everyday....to become or to remain anti-racist: request that your organization, institution, company, corporation, workplace, etc....hire Black top & middle level executives or top managerial employees. Yet, whites tend to stay silent...and this silence makes you "racist"

If you are a White teacher or White parent, and your kids attend a certain school....and you never speak up for or advocate for....the hiring of more & more Black teachers....then you are not anti-racist.... you are a racist

Message to Blacks: it's almost impossible for Blacks to become racists; however, do not try to assimilate to the point that you risk becoming "racist like" or "racist-ish". The value of a dollar is not more important than the value of your spiritual soul...nor is it greater than the love of "self"

Again, the world's conversation is not whether one is racist....the question is this: are you being anti-racist? We only need those who are anti-racist to fight for freedom, justice, and equality

Learn from past events....but only spend about 0.00003 of your energies to regret past events; focus instead....90% of your energies on what's in front of you; use the remaining balance of the 10% on whatever you wish (as long as those things are positive events, tasks, positive fun, occurrences, etc.)

It's easy to love yourself when you are winning....but you should love yourself 3 times more when you are stumbling, falling, or losing too; never give up on you....because I never gave up on you...never

Does it really take an extraordinary woman to be better than any woman at all? Yes! Simply put....if she is not extraordinary, let her go....quickly or slowly....say bye to her but never say bye to any kids that you create...never

Let's talk "street" for a second; pussy is never the prize; pussy is only designed for momentary pleasure; real pleasure is your ability to turn your ideas & thoughts into something positive that other sisters & brothers around you can use to better themselves; therefore.... knowledge is the true pleasure & prize. If she is not about the business of improving the family's knowledge....kick her to the curve

Somewhere in old proverbs: don't give your monies & strength to a woman....they have destroyed Kings....as paraphrased in 31:3....just google it

Hello my children....how are you....I just wanted to feel the blood in your hands....have a great day & a great tomorrow too...I love you

Stay aware of those good or evil people who attempt to create an algorithm that arbitrarily amplifies one or a few selective moments of your greatness or weaknesses (street version: "watch out for haters of all kind....because those fools will try to break you or trip you up.... plus, those fools don't know who you truly "is"....dang, I thought they knew"). Evil lurks or hide behind goodness quite often....stay alert & stay mindful (you owe evil.... nothing)

When an individual, group, institution, or organization of any kind turns their back on you....just make sure to keep your character, integrity, composure & focus....and show them this word via your mature & self-loving actions: enough! Focus on you & your goals.... and continue to love yourself....all while moving forward one step at a time....one foot in front of the other one. Nothing more & nothing less....because you are extremely special & important to me....and to yourself as well

I spent plenty of wonderful years molding you into what I thought you wanted to be. Then, I quickly realized that it is my honor & pleasure to take a huge step back...to watch you reveal & to become who you wanted to be....and I truly honor & respect that realization & revelation. It's an honor to watch you doing you! Thank you for teaching me too!

Where there is truth....there's strength; guard your strength via maintaining your truth

Dad & Mom always emphasized that 'smart work & common sense beats hard work....and due diligence beats intelligence everytime'. I say this: "they are right & they remain the wisest parents who ever lived"

You are what I dreamt; you are my constant thoughts; you are my thoughts & dreams; succeed on with your dreams my child; you are what I constantly dream it would be; you are everything that I thought you would be; simply thinking of you is so awesome!

Know this....I did not create you with an expiration date....nor did I ever put an expiration date on your dreams; your dreams solely belong to you; your dreams can come true at any age. Do not put an expiration date on your goals, missions, tasks, or dreams....there's no expiration date so as long as you have oxygen in your heart, mind, body, and soul. That Davis' blood never expires! Never!

Life is like a musical instrument: don't rush it, don't fear it, don't get too frustrated or too depressed with it....just take your time to breathe....and just hit the right note. Trust your training! More importantly, trust yourself! In life, even if you play the wrong note.... quickly find the right key or just the right note & keep playing! Just play the right note. There you go....you did it....you got it! That's the right note! Now that you have mastered that particular instrument of life....learn a new one....or a new technique or style. Stay coachable.... keep smiling on the inside & outside....you got this! Just keep-on keeping-on! I trust you....so continue to trust yourself....play the right note & just keep playing!!!

At some point in your wonderful life, write your story & then tell your story. Your story should be the most important & the best book that you have ever read. Why? Because at some point you will embrace your differences, you will love your differences even more, and you will continue to love yourself more & more as well. All of these actions represent the importance of "loving & embracing" the magnificent you! You are indeed the most important ingredient of success....in this world's recipe

Perspective! Keep all of life & it's actions & inactions....in its proper form, sense, tense, place, space, & perspective!

Get rid of negative people and negative energies....to include gossip or bad news. Filter all bad vibes or information through these filters: 1) is the information important to my spirituality, 2) is the info helpful or useful in the accomplishments of my goals, 3) can I trust the info & the person, 4) why did the person share this info with me (for growth purposes or just to be messy). Listen to everything....but let your heart keep only the info that's useful

Facing your friends, foes, or enemies: cut ties with any person or group of people who mistreat you, hate you, dislike you, mislead you, misrepresent you, give up on you, etc. Then, in short order, cut ties with that part of yourself that allowed it to happen to you. For example, if your silence caused you to not receive a promotion at work, then you should cut ties with your silence....and standup & speak out! Then, and only then, will you immediately continue your journey towards truly maturing in & growing deeper in....self-love & wisdom! The journey is a continuous process....true change takes time to become part of your character....don't rush it

At the end of day....I have already validated you....therefore, do not allow your validation to depend on some else's silly, racists, childish, sexist, sexual, religious, crazy, or evil expectations of you; your validation is all about your expectations of self....yours & not their's! I validate you each & every day! It's done! You are already validated! Brother man, you are a King....& sister woman, you are a Queen! No one can complete you but you! Only you....can complete you!

Be still....and talk aloud to yourself every morning, every afternoon, and every night....be still for 2 to 3 minutes to allow your great thoughts & energies to flow back to the top of your calm space

Let's be very honest....wish evil to disappear....let that trifling person or persons step....devil be gone regardless of who the person is or pretends to be. As my granddad constantly said, "Devil be gone.... get out of my time & space". It's okay to wish them well....& you do not have to color between the lines anymore. You decide what this great piece of art (you) will look like at the different stages of the process....no one else deserves that power over you. You are your greatest & most valuable piece of art!

Try to live your life while being led by this central question: if I die in 1 year, what are three things that I must do? My answer for me: 1) continue to be an outstanding father to my kids, 2) continue be a great son, brother, uncle, friend, neighbor, etc., and 3) speak truth to power & fight injustices, inequalities, & other evils

Continue to walk in your greatness; teach in your greatness; execute in your greatness; lead in your greatness; walk in your greatness; perform in your greatness; compose in your greatness; write in your greatness; dunk in your greatness; run in your greatness; referee in your greatness; own a business in your greatness; pray in your greatness and etc. I put the greatness inside of you....and it still shines greatly & brightly; I taught you! I validated you! I love you!

If God truly made you & me in his image....and I trust that He did.... then you & I are already Masters of this Universe. Please understand, daily, how great you are....and how great I am. We are the greatest!!! Watch those who will try to piss on your greatness or piss on mine's

Regardless of how many faults, or negative actions that you share with me now or in the future....I will continue to love you unconditionally. I will never use what you share with me....against you or against your heart either. You can communicate to me about anything, big or small....I got you....and I will continue to always love you.....unconditionally

I gave you a pen early in life....now go forth and write your on script, your own play, your own story; no one else has my permission to use your pen....nor can they ever write your story either; write your own story and the rest of the world will be in awe of your greatness

Lessons learned from our miscues, missteps, or misfortunes are indeed our greatest source of energies & remarkable wisdom. True wisdom derives from lessons learned & then using those lessons to solve future problems

Continue to love people but "correct" them too. Just remember that "correction" is okay.... correction is love too....

Try to "stay present" in all that you do. Present means this: don't live your life in the past or the future....because the "present" is the most powerful place to be. Enjoy the power of this moment & also enjoy the power of this specific day. Being present also means to speak your truth, say what's on your mind, say what's inside your heart; say all these things & more....in your own unique way....as tactfully & politely as possible....regardless of your audience. Let's be one hundred percent honest....it's okay to look in the rearview mirror.... just don't live there!

"Well enough" should never be left alone....overly supervise or monitor the bad, the good, the ugly....and spot check the "well enoughs"

An average mind would conclude, “that’s too long....it will take me 5 years to accomplish this.” A great mind mind would say, “let’s accomplish this goal, because the next 5 years are going to occur anyways.” Therefore, every two years, do something to advance your greatness....to elevate your family & love ones, or to make you better!

Elevate people means to inspire them; help your love ones to change various mindsets which could allow them to overcome certain speed bumps or disparities

Each morning....I would say the same thing to my children: "morning & how did you sleep....take about 5 minutes, you need another 10 minutes....bet, pray & then get dressed from head-to-toes, and I love you". This was by designed & not by mistake....it was done purposefully & artfully to prepare you for battle & the battles of life. Prayer + getting fully dress + knowing that I love you = being armored for daily battles & the battles of life. You are equipped for every battle that you will face. The world will throw stones or rocks at you in an effort to dent your armour....but they can never destroy you....because I built you that way....purposefully, pointedly, tactically, strongly, & mercifully. You are ready for battle! Just do not forget to relax & rest along your journey too; choose your battles & then turn your focus to winning the war....not just the battle!

You can sometimes allow others to win little skirmishes or battles.... you just make sure that you win the war!

Facing adversity or struggling mentally: go to sleep around the same time, wake up with a prayer, conduct your personal hygiene, put on your clothes, put on your shoes, tighten up your shoe laces & say rrrrroooofffff. Now that you have on your true armor, you are ready to face the world & any problems in the world

The purpose of tightening up your shoe laces every morning: because there will be different battles to fight or different problems to solve every day. You may have to walk, you may have to jog, you may have to run or sprint....you just may have to do a military-high crawl or low crawl tactic....but you have every tool at your disposal to fight every battle. Trust your instincts....and get up & get dressed....from head-to-toes....and stay safe at all times (you are now "battle-ready")

Here's the secret sauce after getting fully dressed: sit & develop 2 or 3 different "courses of actions" to each problem or challenge....choose the best course of action or the best one that makes the most sense at that time; once you make the decision....own it & live with it. That's the real secret....but you have to pray & get fully dressed first....you cannot go into battle without putting on your armour....given to you from your earthly father

3 choices when disaster occurs: hide, fight, or sprint. For example, if there is a shooting at the school, church, club, neighborhood, or any local establishment, you have to quickly decide to duck or hide, fight back, or sprint away. Let me share a nonviolent story with you. During my high school sophomore year, I was chosen to run the 1-mile run for our track & field team....and I would usually finish in the top three at most track meets. Yet, during this particular meet, I fell down on the last lap....and once you fall down....you lose great momentum. At that moment, I had to make a quick decision to hide my face from the crowd & teammates, get up and fight with determination, or get up and sprint my hardest toward the finish line. I chose to get up and sprint toward the finish line! Why? Because one of the greatest lessons in life is to finish the race! Of course, I did not finish in the top 3....and that lost hurt like hell for years....and it still hurts, a little, to this very day....but I finished. Yes, it did hurt....but I finished! I finished!

Did it happen "to you"....or....did it happen "for you"? It = anything good or bad. This is the central question that we must ask ourselves as soon as disaster strikes

When trouble happens....then immediately determine two things: 1) is it the beginning or the end of your life, 2) what meaning or value will you assign to it (only list your positive meaning....not someone else's negative meaning), and 3) how much do you value "your value" & self worth

Knowing your value means: this is “what I know” I can do versus “what you demand” that I do, this is what I brought to the table, this is how I want to feel everyday, I represent goodness, I share positive energies with you & others, I constantly give these 3 positive characteristics to you; I know that I am valuable to the right person in the right situation, etc. This is not the right situation to honor my value....nor to honor my values....my father gave me my values & I will not prostitute any of my values just to satisfy your thirst....I deserve better! I will continue to reach for & grab “better” as well

Always be willing to separate or divorce yourself from anything positive....or from anything negative as well. The word "anything" also includes any person who lives on planet earth. Any person!!!

Be extremely careful of this word called "loyalty". When should you stop being loyal to anybody? As soon as your loyalty is "disloyal" to you & disloyal to your entire existence....and to your way of just being. Stay grounded and don't allow others to steer you away from your truths nor your values. Please note & believe that none of the "Earth's Whores" are loyal....so I caution you to stay true to yourself....and to let those who are not loyal....do what they do. Remember, none of these whores are loyal!!!

Real world or reality: some days you will want to pull the covers over your head....it's okay. It's okay to take a day off to recuperate & to breathe. By the next day....stay consistent with your rituals of starting your day with prayer & getting dressed....because if you would just stay consistent....you will always get back on track with accomplishing your goals. Pray, rest, study, train, work, lead, invest, entertain, have fun, rest again, etc....but most importantly, stay consistently consistent!

Consumers versus producers: don't just spend monies or become so consumed with monies; make your monies work for you (own rental properties, etc.), and focus more on creating more monies. Focus more on sharing your talents & gifts with the world....versus being focused on spending monies or just working a non-interesting or lame job....anybody can work a job....chase your passion....work your passion....whether it makes you rich or poor....continue to share your talents mundanely....and the riches will come

When you become dead serious about success....look to find you a business partner who understands & appreciates the value of losing. This is applicable in your social life as well. Quickly identify those individuals who only want to hang with when you are winning.... those people are useless to your long-term goals. What are those people going to do when the lights get cutoff? The ones who do not appreciate the lessons of "lights off"....will never truly appreciate the value of "lights on" either

The greatest fathers on earth, like me, always made sure that he provided his kids 5 things: you are healthy & fed, happy & loved, trained & educated, adored & appreciated, and finally, the father always communicated pertinent suggestions & quality reminders

I appreciate you = you give me so much value!

Live in the moment without disregarding your past....think & plan for the future....but live that day....and on tomorrow, live tomorrow during tomorrow

While I am living, I will probably do most of the talking. Yet, I promise you this much....once I transition to my final resting place, you can do all the talking to me & I will do the listening

Daily advice for each and every day of your life....ask for help and then accept the help....on each & everything regardless of how big or small the task. Ask for help. Why? By accepting the help....it gives you a wonderful opportunity to meet someone new, interesting, and different. It also presents a unique opportunity for us to set aside our egos....just for a moment. Ask for help....it's a beautiful thing & gesture

In case you are wondering, your competitive colleagues, co-workers, friends, classmates, etc....will never "out compete you". Why? Because they do not "know" the meaning of grind & sacrifice....nor will they ever sacrifice the same things that you have sacrificed to get to where you are now. Embrace that, know that, and trust that! Also, if you want to win at any competition, start by outworking your competition, preparing better, studying better, briefing better, listening better, gaining better skills, gaining better mentorship, obtaining better knowledge & skills, improving your networking capabilities & abilities, being the most dependable & reliable teammate, being the most timely, and sharing your integrity, values, character, & leadership traits with those willing participants. Generally speaking, these are all of the "starters" that you will need to compete successfully. There are no shortcuts to this process.... do the aforementioned steps....and stay competitive through every scenario....

True love is this (earthly wise)....who do I want wiping my bottom while on my sick bed (in other words....who do I want caring for me in my greatest time of physical, emotional, or mental weakness or distress....who do I trust the most....to treat me like I request to be treated?)

Always release your intelligence, your brilliance, and your talent. If heaven is the highest point that you can go, I have already told you....to go higher! You do not have to worry about impressing people....just release your brilliance & talent....so that you will leave an impact of excellence on this world. You are the epitome of impact & excellence!!!

My Dad and Mom gave me a ton of fortunes & all the riches of this world....even while the world attempted to minimize their greatness or tried to cap their earning power to just the value of a single dime.... but the evil people of the world lost. Along that same accord, there is no other race of people who can overcome evil & make things work & stretch....like my parents did throughout their lives; my kids are the direct descendants of perseverance, honor, & truth; I am truly honored, blessed, and extremely grateful for all of my riches; I am so fortunate to stand on their shoulders. Thank you for instilling values in my heart, mind, body, & soul....it made me the richest man in the world!!!

Racism = evil; racism is also the greatest form of internal & external evil; evil cannot stop your dreams; evil will not & cannot win in the end; persevere far beyond racism and let your light shine brighter & brighter; accomplish "your" dreams

You are in charge of your own light....no one can extinguish your flames....no one

If you want better treatment from friends, colleagues, family members, etc....stop training them to treat you in a disrespectful or negative manner. For example, if friends or others are calling you at late hours when you are trying to rest or study....they are doing it because you keep answering the phone calls or texts; if people are always begging for a ride or borrowing your monies....it's because you are giving them a free ride or you keep their pockets filled....but they do not care about how broke you might be or what financial struggles you may be facing momentarily; if the friends keep on seeking your counsel because you are a great listener & fixer....you are at fault because you keep training those friends with your quick & positive availability. Stop and say "no" to all of the distractions that will prevent you from being great! Slowly but surely....keep eliminating bad people of all shapes & sizes. The best way to this end: keep practicing the word "no"....& stop training people to perfect their bad habits onto you

If I practice saying "no"....there's no ceiling as to how much I could grow; say no....to everybody....it's healthy....and necessary

There will come plenty of times that you will catch yourself playing the role of "fool". We all have played & started as a lead actor or actress in several of those movies. It's okay....just sit in silence and slow your heart rate a bit....then text or call the person or persons and say.... "I can no longer support your habits....because I am going to focus more on my goal attainment, mental stability, & myself. I have nothing but love for ya....but I must move forward. Thanks"!

If it ain't one thang....then it's a nutta. But here's the catch....focus on fixing that one thang that happened first....then focus on the nutta. Fix or focus on one thing at a time....you are not a robot....you are a beautiful, well-oiled, human being

We don't live life....but we survive life; I just want to live life to it's fullest for at least one day....just one day....to experience that spiritual high....one day is all I ask

I chose to teach you English & Math for a plethora of reasons....but none more important than the following statements. Math & English will always command the room.... regardless of the chosen room. By being an expert at Math, you immediately know that every problem, for the most part, is very solvable. Therefore, every problem has solution. Just breathe, gather the right formula....and solve for X, Y, or Z. Life is full of mathematical variables & challenges galore.... do not fear it....just relax, breathe, & respectfully solve it. Here's the other secret: sometimes you may have to revisit problem #3 after you have worked 70 problems. It's okay....just put a little tick mark by #3....and if you have enough space & time on your fault calendar.... give problem #3 another look. Problem solved....all problems solved! Don't be discouraged....because there are more problems in the next chapter as well. You may be anxious or a little nervous but you are not afraid....because you know how to solve life's problems

Here's a different take on problems. Be thankful of all and any problems, learn from those problems, and then embrace the failures that are attached to those problems. Why? If you lose a parent, at least you had some years with that parent; if you lost a friend....then you probably had some real good times with that friend; if you had to change jobs....at least you had a job at some point in your life; if you lost a house....at least you were never homeless; if you cannot have children....then you can adopt from a pool of millions of kids across the world; if you lost your hair, at least you had a head full of hair to lose; if you have experienced hatred of any form....you also have experienced love too. My point is this: bad moments & failures will occur....just look for the positive moments of those bad situations....but learn all the meaningful lessons associated with those bad situations. Here's a question that I always asked myself when bad things happened: how can I use these lessons to improve me & the people around me? Things are not normally "bad" until we react in a terrible or negative manner toward the "bad"....or show a certain range of emotions while responding to the "bad". Put another way, is the glass half-empty or half-full? Since you have Davis' blood....the glass is always half-full....because we are problem solvers

If I take a picture of any group, organization, classroom, grade, class, or workplace, and I showed you that picture....what is the first thing that you will do with that picture? You will probably look at the picture & then attempt to find yourself in that picture. If you find yourself in that picture, you will begin to smile, rejoice, and walk with a certain degree of pride. You would probably say, "look at me....I am so handsome or beautiful. Right? However, if you do not see yourself in that same picture, your first question would probably be "where am I?" When you do not see yourself in the picture or group, you will probably feel sad, depressed, or a little down in the dumps. This is the exact reason why our schools & workplaces are screwed up in this country....and this is why our school systems do not work effectively. Furthermore, when we do not see ourselves in the "picture", those same invisible people do not give it their all or best & the students' best talents are almost impossible to unlease. Sons, daughters, students, employees, business owners, volunteer members, and others....should always feel inclusive....and only then will they release their true talents & patriotism. Families, institutions, organizations, churches, etc...have to be inclusive & celebratory in everything involving our children.... regardless of their age, race, sexual orientation, politics, political agenda, religion, beliefs, etc.

On this day....what are you doing for you? What special thing are you doing solely for yourself?

Set aside at least one hour per day to do something special for yourself (rest, yoga drills, meditation, write, breathing deeply, long shower, long bath, manicure, pedicure, haircut, etc.). Never forget about yourself!!!

Putting yourself first....and being "selfish"....are two separate & different thoughts; take care of #1....you are always #1 on your list, schedule, or daily routine

Alot of young folks are experiencing "rejection"....and those feelings of rejection could lead to major depression. When experiencing any form of rejection, please do the following: 1) know that you are very important to me & you do not owe anybody....anything; release any negative thoughts in a healthy way, 2) talk with a professional or a trusted individual on a monthly basis, 3) increase your professional talks & conversations if needed, 4) speak openly to other individuals, who are close to you, and talk about how you are truly feeling, and finally, 5) tell people when you need a minute to breathe....plus tell them when you just need to take some time for yourself....to just mediate & regather your thoughts & feelings.

Try to make yourself the priority every morning....even if you have to get up an hour or two before the kids, grandkids, friends, wife, spouse, roommate, colleagues, etc....or even before the pet-animals

Why do you have to be the priority? Because....if you are flying on an airplane, you have to be able to put on your "oxygen mask" first....before putting the mask on your kids or the other passengers. Put your mask on first....then give others all the help & assistance in the world

Do not wrestle with simple decisions; if the decision is not a life or death one....then it's simple. You should always "sleep on" most major decisions....but don't allow those decisions to become overly stressful or burdensome in nature.

Since everybody has a story....know yourself inside & out....and stay ready to share your story with the world. Get ready "world"....my kids will make an effective impact throughout your land

Two important pieces of advice to do daily: 1) think outside the box, and 2) continue to be an adult (physically, mentally, spiritually, emotionally, etc.)....but always be a child at heart. What does this means to be "a child at heart"? It means that a child always ask questions every minute of the day! For example, Dad, why is the sky blue? Dad, where are we going? Dad, how do I work this Math problem? Dad, why can't I sit upfront in the passenger's seat? Dad, why do I have to go to sleep right now? Dad, do I have to do homework right now? You see....the typical younger kid stays hungry....and a kid is always willing to learn something new....or trying to make incremental improvements. Yet, most adults think that they know everything....until there is a problem or a disaster! Be an Adult....but stay a Kid at heart! Always ask questions....improve yourself....while learning something new!

Serendipity happens most frequently....especially when we take one small step outside of our comfort zone....and say hi or hello

Don't be afraid to introduce yourself; when introducing yourself, start with your name....then ask two friendly questions....then follow those two questions with two interesting statements as well. Now you have a great start to a "conversation".... personally & professionally speaking....it works

Quality vs Longevity of life. What if God offered you quality of life versus longevity of life. Which one would you take? What if both are the same? They are! Why? Because God will never make known your last day on earth. Now, which one would you take?

General career advice: just seek the next-best opportunity

Do not allow the world to speak negatively of your father or dad.... because they are not worthy. You know that I am the greatest & you also know the great things (big & small) that I have done for you & that I will continue to be there for you as long as breath is in my lungs

Most people say evil or mean-spirited things to hide their own sins or inequities; never forget that you sit on top of a mountain and you have the unique ability to "ignore" or "overlook" their degrees of ignorance or evil. Just smile & ignore those negative folks who are trying to steal your thunder, calmness, & joy; you sit with the Most High....and will always "overlook" or look down upon negative folks & all negative things

When negative people confront you with mean or ugly things.... just say something similar to this: "thank you....but I see it very differently". When you encounter negative folks in the countryside, just say, "thank you....but that dog won't hunt". When you encounter negative folks in the urban area, say this: "thank you....but I'm good my brother or my sister". For all others, just say, "thank you....I appreciate your suggestions....and I will consider all of them"

Let's be honest....because there will be times that you will also have to tell folks: "backup & stop fucking with me". Then, you should immediately take 3 deep breaths....and move out smartly & safely

Do not feel bad about telling folks how you truly feel. Yes, even in casual conversations....you will probably feel a little guilty....just breathe and then stand by your honest feelings. There is no need to "take back" honesty

While on your road to success, you will meet alot of people....some good & some bad....some super intelligent & and some not so much. The key is this: do not allow people who are not going somewhere in life....take you with them; carefully choose your friends & other folks....because evil always love one thing: company

There is a God: God, God, and God....

Mathematically speaking....love who you love....but marriage is not the sums of 1 + 1....nor is marriage a result....nor the right economic solution to any linear equation; do not do it young man....do not do it young woman

My young men....surrogacy is better than having an abortion; plan for & then choose surrogacy & take full custody of your child or children; instill that manly confidence in each of your children & bring them up the right way....without a ratchet or a selfish female always in the discussion; show up & stay accountable my young men

There is a big difference between being selfish versus "self" full. Fill yourself with goodness....and erase all negativity via "just dating".... but never marrying

Understanding "hurt" versus "hurtful" feelings. People in your circle or outside of your circle may say something that you perceived as hurtful. For example, parents will definitely say, "that plan may not be the best decision". The children hear this: "my parents don't understand me & they think that I do not have a brain & my parents do not like my choices". Meanwhile, what the kids should have heard is this: "I do not dislike you, the kid, I just disagree with that particular choice because it does not sound very safe". Additionally, most parents want two things from their kids when sharing guidance with their kids: parents want listening & parents want to know that you will be stable & safe. Therefore, most parents only intend to be helpful....and at times their messages will appear, on the surface, to be hurtful....but most parents never intend for their messages to send "hurt" to their kids. True parents do not send out "hurt". All parents need to improve communication with their kids....and all kids should quickly know that most parents only want the best for their children. The quicker that kids understand how to "repackage" every message, from every sender, the quicker they will be ready to deal with difficult people throughout the world.

Parents across every spectrum: grow up, listen to your kids, repackage your message before you speak it, remove negative emotions from your hearts & tongues, tamper your lofty expectations, allow your kids to have their own dreams and expectations, stay stable, stay calm, stay cool, & listen some more....and even then some. Children desire these things from their parents at a minimum: love, listening, support, safe haven, safe space, and stability. Again just listen to your kids....and then have them to define these things to you in an effort to increase your understanding. Our kids are our best teachers.... allow them to teach you!

Just listen to me now

I don't believe in this phrase echoing or highlighting, "if it's not broke, then don't fix it". I say this: if it's not broke....then make it better....just make improvements to it. Always leave it better than we found it....that's what true leaders do

Embrace rejection; sometimes you have to be rejected in order to gain acceptance for yourself. For example, if you were trying to ask a girl out on date, you should be happy if she says no. Why? Mathematically speaking, one rejection means that there are three acceptances waiting for you. Think of it as attending or being at a party....or the club. Most guys will not walk up & ask the girl to dance because they are scared of being rejected. No sir! Embrace the rejection! We should want to be rejected at least 10 times that night. Why? Because that means you probably will dance with 20+ other girls, or it means that you got 20+ phone numbers. Dating is a "mindset" thing....just change your outlook & embrace rejection with a smile. Rejection will always lead to something or someone better....even if "better" does not happen very quickly. This concept works in the business, corporate, church, or school world too. Embrace rejection! Something better is awaiting you! Move on to the next-best thing!

Encountering trouble or just negative situations: decide whether you will "step out" or "step away". Stepping out means that you will probably just take a quick break & then go back to do the same bad habits. Stepping away means that you will not allow trouble to follow you & you will not bring that trouble into your new environment. It truly means that you have washed your hands of trouble from that group of friends, individuals, colleagues, or situations. Make sure that trouble is not on the inside of you. If trouble is on the inside of you.... it will follow you wherever you go. Get rid of all forms of trouble!

One way to get rid of trouble: daily prayer + actions! Here is the long equation: prayer + stepping away + quitting it cold turkey + plugging something positive in the gaps or places

My dad used to say, "if you fall off the horse, get back on it immediately...only then would you have succeeded". Here is a more modern-day take on what he was saying: failure is only real when you do not get back up; if you get back up....then you automatically win; if you want to continue winning....just reassess your actions, take an inventory of all your lessons learned, and do it better & better....the next few times. Now, you have moved from "win" to "constantly winning"....to "have won"! However, here is the catch: do not allow "won" to be your end-state or your end-goal....keep making improvements on you....make you better!

Thieves appear as friends and will continue to surround that wonderful person who always give & give & give of himself; the thieves are the ones who constantly take & take & take....while never realizing that they are robbing you of the very ingredients & nutrients needed to fulfill your daily missions; thieves also never realize the scope of your daily sacrifices & your willingness to be there for them & available to each & every person; thieves are highly selfish! They are everywhere! They hide in relationships, they are at school, church, work, fun places, etc. Thieves do not deserve your goodness! They are not worthy....

When this happens....and you become sick & tired of being sick & tired....just rise up and say, "I love you....but enough! I am no longer going to empty my proverbial gas tank just to give you free gas from my spiritual tank every day....enough! It's time for me to enjoy my own full tank of gas....instead of feeling empty or drained along My Tour of Life....enough!" I love you....but I love God & myself more!!!

It's okay to chase greener pastures....or to go to the other side because it's greener....however, before you make the move....just make sure that the "green" is not merely "water"....or a mirage-effect

When starting your business, don't ever be afraid of earning small monies occasionally....because small monies could turn into big monies; just remember that even a penny can be invested & turned into millions of dollars

Too much credit....is just as bad as none at all; pay cash for the overwhelming majority of your purchases; build your home out of your pocket; buy your future vehicles under your business line of credit; hire & consult with an accountant; study, watch, & monitor your accounts, transactions, & your monies; consult with different accountants; always keep all transactions & other actions above board; stay honest

Protect your "yes" and use a whole lot of "no"....this is the true daily balance toward "a sound mind, body, & soul"

While checking on your "mentals"....I'm checking on my "mentals" too; my "mentals" are at its strongest....when yours are too

Stress vs peace: don't allow your stress to interrupt your peace....or your peace to intertwine with your stress; this is a delicate balancing act...yet it truly should be a part of our daily diet

Daily stretches, daily pushups, daily situps, and a daily yoga-like activity to focus on breathing & stretching....to stay heart healthy & stress free....plus add any other activities twice weekly (church, softball, frisbee, flag football, skating, movies, dancing, etc.)

"Give out" but never "give up" (you can get too tired....but just put one foot in front of the other....and never stop marching forward). Even if you have to take a long break (giving out)....just try to finish what needs to be finished (never giving up). Get up & get dressed.... and lace up your shoes....now we are ready to face whatever life throws at us.... let's go-get-em

Know the difference between a fried green tomato vs. a fried red tomato (there's no difference because it's the same tomato....someone just "picked" the green tomato off the vine....before it turned red). We can solve 90% of life's problems....if only we would focus on "not waiting for the tomato to turn red"

You can look back....but only look back after you crossed the finished line....or after you have just accomplished your task or mission for the day. Yet, it's okay to take a peep....and admire what you have accomplished. It's okay....

Sometimes people have to hear you growl & roar like a lion....and only then will they realize & appreciate that you were only showing them your lamb's gifts of intelligence, kindness, brilliance, calmness, & patience

Be careful of those group of females masquerading as real women who always say, "I don't need a man." Yes they do! The problem is that those same women are angry at themselves and angry at their own problems & ways of life. Those same females (Black or White) are also angry at our Black Men for sharing our truths....and they are angry for men being brutally honest with ourselves & brutally honest to our women. Women ask for honesty....but cannot handle truths! When men give women their honesty....women mostly likely use it against him. At that moment, that particular man becomes quiet, distant, nonchalant, non-intimate, unresponsive, etc. Then, the female wonders why we will not talk with her & share our truths with her any longer. Because we can no longer trust her with our valuable & in-depth thoughts. Also, please note that those same women are trying to be & act like men as well. Let similar women, like her, walk! Don't fall for her tactics ...just let her step or let her keep walking far away from you You remain & stay a man! Don't lose confidence of who you truly are. You are a Man! You deserve better & you also deserve a better quality or a better grade of a woman. Don't allow any female or woman to place you into her "trick bag". Make sure that she's the trick! Let that bitch step!!!

The main thing a woman need to know about a man: the man will only be interested & stay interested in the relationship when he feels needed. If he is told directly or indirectly that he is not needed....or that she can do 'this or that' by herself....then the female just lost him. He will then allow her the room & space to "hang herself". This is the epitome of why "every word" is so very powerful....

Also, be careful of that "corporate or work whore" who prostituted herself just to break-up the family structure. She did it by saying, "I want to work outside of the home....and put my kids last". Because of this phenomenon....the home is broken before the child is even born. She will prostitute herself to a corporation or a job....over her kids, just to make that "almighty dollar". Then, when you remind her to follow her leader (the Man)....she will give you every excuse as to why she does not follow. Excuses such as these: "he does not go to church," "he yells" (but she yells 100 times more per month), "he won't work," "he does work," "he cheats with other women," etc. None of the aforementioned excuses have anything to do with leading your household or leading your relationship. Men should Lead....and Females should follow! When that dynamic is not adhered to....the household is out-of-whack or out-of-alignment

My dad & granddad would say, "mind your head, heart, hands, and feet". This was his way of saying that one should "guard" those four things and use all four of them to watch out for daily danger

Simple things that we take for granted, seemingly everyday, include: giving thanks to God & others, giving thanks for just making it home, being healthy, being able to attend to the wants of nature, having all our senses, and the list continues

If you can see it, taste it, or dream it....you can achieve it. So, again, what is the question?

At some point in your life, you will probably feel like you cannot go on, or you may feel like your options are limited; when you feel like that....press on; get dressed; you are not stuck....you just decided to stay in the proverbial fight; you always have viable options; when you have great options....you are never stuck; the key is to identify those viable options....quickly & responsibly. That's the solution!

Committed Relationships: ask yourself this question before commiting to any person.... "what do I want from this person that I cannot give to myself"? Sex? You can get that from a whore or a prostitute....or a legit chick. Money? You have your own "bank" and you do not need her's. Cleaning? Clean it yourself or hire a maid once per week. Cooking? Use your own monies to "eat out" on the town or hire a "soul-food cooker" to come in and cook two or three times weekly. Lawncare? Hire a landscaping & lawncare company to maintain your yard. Managing all the bills? You manage all your own bills & take advantage of paying all of your bills online in an effort to save you from running around the nostalgic way. Dropping off or picking up the kids from daycare or school? Always dropoff & pickup your own child. However, when you need a little help....just call the Nanny who just hired. I can go on & on....but you get the point. Again, "what do I want from this person that I cannot give to myself"? Answer: nothing!

Very kindly & sweetly....I ask, "who are you?". Describe yourself.... to yourself, at least once per month; get to know you a little better.... this is most important

Separate your needs from your wants....then decrease all of the above to "your gotta-have's;" when a man has his gotta have's....he does not need a "thang"

When putting in tough-smart work, you can expect great results; when you put in no work or average work....expect an average result; don't get frustrated when you know that you have not put in the tough-smart work

Keep on playing the game of chess & mastering chess. Why? I taught you this game to teach you about life. Just because the world steals a piece of yours, take an important or insignificant piece, etc. You do not have to get so excited or angry....and take one of their pieces. Instead, focus on the grand plan of "establishing checkmate". Moral of these teaching points: control your emotions, control your thirst, and focus on your desired outcome....your "end game"....not theirs....

While you are guarding your heart, don't forget to guard your peace & quiet too

Society has labeled «divorce» an ugly word. Yet, I say that divorce is a beautiful word....when used in a healthy way. For example, divorce should be used in all personal relationships, in all business relationships, in all academic relationships, in all church relationships, etc. When a person walks away....that's courage....not weakness! It takes courage to find your inner voice, to find your inner peace, and to find your inner spirits. Divorce is courage....not a weakness! Don't be afraid to divorce the world....when you need to find you! It takes courage to walk away....courage!

Push past the hate from idiots; you have too much to lose; don't spend your positive energy chasing their fallacies; read or research the 5 logical fallacies used in political & policy debates....to really understand haters' endgame

Idiots come in all shapes & sizes; idiots sometimes include family, friends, mentors, church folks, deacons, pastors, teachers, and other trusted counsel as well; be aware

Forgiveness takes a long time & comes in two parts: forgive the other person or persons....then also forgive the most important person.... yourself

No matter your age, no matter what you go through at different stages in your life....please know that somebody cares about you; someone cares enough to offer you quality advice, a helping hand, or a nice hug....somebody cares! I am just one of those "somebodies"

In most debates, briefings, arguments, or discussions, practice the 3 B's: be brilliant....be brief....be gone

If one thinks that the world's adoption of this concept called "The Holy Bible" is going to solve his or her Problems....then, he or she doesn't know anything about the Bible....nor his or her Problems either

Regardless of where you are in life....once you have reached the 7th grade....have a plan....and always know where you are trying "to go" in your life; if you have to make strategical adjustments along the route....it's perfectly okay....it's part of planning

One of my greatest strengths & values: I continue to love you every single second of every single day. Even when I disagree or disapprove of a specific task or action, I will never stop loving you; my love for you is....and will always be permanent

Get into the arena; get into the room.... appreciate what you have done....then own the entire damn arena, building, room, and other spaces

Own real estate....and rent it to tenants for rental income....which will enhance your current, future, & retirement income; make those dollars work for you

As you continue to live life to it's fullest....don't fall "in love"....just "love" & demand love in return. The concept of "in love" only surrounds itself with infatuation, make-believe, momentary, chasing, etc. On the other hand, "love" does not change with the winds, it does not refuse kindness or a caring spirit; "love" is an embedded attitude that remains steadfast....regardless of what is happening around that person. I know this one thing: I love you!

There are 3 sides to every coin; always determine 3 courses of actions or options before making most of your big decisions

Don't act bad or be bad....just keep the bad ones off you (just walk away as calmly as possible); it takes a real man to walk from danger.... or to just walk away period

Treat anger, madness, frustration like a bitch, i.e., that is, treat all three of them like a "dog" & just escort your "three dogs" on a short walk everyday....to relieve stress

Why I never liked dogs? I disklike any animal that ignorant folks treat better than they treat People of Color. The 2nd Golden Rule should be "to treat all people better than we treat animals."

I heard that....that you heard this

When the world complains about crime being too high....please remind them that crime will never cease until all people have the same access to education, obtain a good education, access to the same capital, access to the same hidden capital system, and have economic inclusion

My most important gift: my two beautiful parents giving birth to me....plus me giving birth via creating my children, plus....my children giving birth and/or creating my future grandkids....and the continuance of this "mission of life"

What is winning? Winning is not just coming in first at an event, performance, or at another venue. Instead, winning is an internal formula consisting of this: your passion + your purpose + your enjoyment + your goal setting + goal accomplishments + eliminating a few distractions = Winning! You already know how to Win! I taught you! You are a Winner....keep on Winning!

Position yourself to win....and always grab a seat at the table. If you cannot grab a seat at the table, then at least enter the building....and when you think the time is just right....take a seat at the table....it's yours.... you've earned it!!

Trouble is akin to the devil & it (trouble) will try to attack you at anytime.... particularly at your highest, lowest, or weakest moments; stay prayed up!

Whenever you need a physical hug and it's unavailable....a spiritual hug has to quickly fill that physical void; pray aloud....whenever a hug, of any type, is needed; I usually pray real loud when I'm driving or just walking to the mailbox

Talk "to" yourself aloud, talk "with" yourself aloud....debate yourself aloud....it's healthy and I talk with myself....because I love talking with intelligent people

Be aware of average people with average intellect....who are innately afraid of your brilliance, presence, & professionalism, who will try desperately through racist actions or hatred...to minimize your accomplishments down to ashes; use those same ashes as your "green fuel" to continue your ascension toward your success; rise & remind them of your brilliance; own the room because it's your damn room

My dad & mom would regularly sing & humm these words: “I ain’t gonna let nobody turn me around”

When I was “knee tall to a June bug”....I asked my parents why they would constantly sing that song....and this is what they said, “I sing to keep from hurting those evil folks who are racists”

Effective time management: it's extremely hard to serve two masters; eliminate the noise around you & simply prioritize....it's just that simple....coupled with applying the daily practice of saying the word... "no"

If you want to know what you like....try something that you don't like....then, try something you don't already know....(of course.... safety first)

Trust your intestinal fortitude (gut) or....your gastrointestinal tract

You are not what others think of you; you are 100 times more important & powerful....than your initial positive thoughts of yourself

You are not who your parents are, you are not who your grandparents are, you are not who your other teachers & mentors are, you are not who your pastor & deacons are, you are not who your ushers are, you are not who your siblings are, your are not who your neighbors are, you are not who your friends & "dates" are, you are not who your future spouses are; you are not who your kids & future kids are, you are "you"....and that's a beautiful person to be; yet....if you like certain traits of anyone mentioned above or....not mentioned above.... then adopt those people's positive traits into your own life, living, & such; borrow those traits and make them yours

Dream, dream, & dream....then do the dreams....

Here's my #1 lesson about love: it's not best "to receive"....its best to give & to receive....because you will definitely grow tired of "giving" all the time....with no reciprocity in clear sight & with no reciprocity in return

Sometimes in life....we have to stop riding the train....and enjoy a good scenic ride on the bus....or just a good walk or jog; slow down young leader....slow down & just breathe in the fresh air; prioritize your "to do list"....daily speaking

If God gave me only 3 wishes to give to my kids....I would gift them: a great head on their shoulders, a great heart, and a great thirst for solving problems in life. I gave you those gifts already....enjoy them and love them

The devil you know....is better than the devil you don't know

Keep your enemies very close to you....and your friends even closer; you will need to know where both groups are when trouble appears.... because you will not be able to tell one from another....at times; stay alert

If you have to be better, smarter, or a more skilled communicator than anyone else in the "room"....know that you already are & just do it; despite the racism, imbalances, inequalities, inequities, hatred, etc....just do it....show them why you are in the "room"

Let your identity be rooted deeply in those values that I have given to you; bloom where you are planted; the world is not only your playground....it's also your canvass & oasis....paint your portrait.... your way

Your identity is not your birthplace, it is not an artificial legacy, occupation, business, job, salary, material things, or big dollars of any kind....your identity is the amount of values and power that you "share with" or "instill in" others....all while honoring your roots.... that's your identity!

Everyday after conducting your personal hygiene, start watering your "garden of life"....but don't forget to water the roots....not just the leaves....but the roots; your roots are the reason that you are alive, successful & well. That Davis' blood runs deep & it waters every root to perfection....everyday!

Always pay yourself first (which means to educate yourself, save, invest, teach, and give wisely); also....even if you have to start small.... own some rental properties, enjoy it, grow it, and pass the properties down to your kids; generational wealth building should be at the cornerstone of your future investments; build it & pass it down to your kids

Respect freedom....love freedom....sing freedom....teach freedom.... live freedom.... facilitate freedom....give freedom....pray freedom

Borrow my heart, borrow my mind, borrow my values; borrow my leadership; borrow my greatness; borrow my confidence; borrow my love; borrow my laughter; borrow my strength; borrow my soul; borrow my ideas, borrow any trait of mine and you will never have to return it; yet, the only debt owed to me is to pay it forward.... and continue to make those traits a valuable part of you and your journey....in & throughout your life

Any trait borrowed from me.... automatically becomes yours

Main career & life advice: go and do you....only do you...try to eventually go where you will be loved, admired, trusted, and appreciated....there is where you will begin to align with «your calling & your passion»....there is where you will find the «riches» of internal peace & internal freedom

How do you do this? secondary career advice: seek the next-best opportunity; you are your best life coach & career manager; identify you 3 or more mentors at every stage of your life & career; alter any and all plans....and again, seek the next-best opportunity

When things seemingly are too tough, when the world seems to question you unfairly, when people question your worth or other values.....what do you do? Just do you....and persevere! Look them squarely in the eyes....and persevere! This is why I am always lamenting, "you belong"....

Persevere = keep on keeping on....change or choose another course of action if needed; don't wallow in misery or stay in a bad situation just to save face or prove a point....trust "your" instincts and not other people's instincts

When talking, speaking, or just plain-old engaging with someone.... always do this: look them eyeballs to eyeballs. My grandad use to say to me, "don't look down....because there is no discharge on the ground". He defined discharge as feces....crap....waste....etc.

Find a little ounce of fun in every task, mission, or activity that you do; finding that "fun" angle....keeps you young forever; stay focused & have some fun

Continue to rise; rise until you are standing "head and shoulders" above the wicked mountains named: cannot, hope, wishing, going to, after while, not yet, fixing to, and other passive articulations; once you have defeated those wicked mountains....pick out you a safe & comfortable area or spot "to just be you"

Let me tell you a secret....you will experience some form of these mountains daily or monthly....just know that you have that "built in will power" to defeat all obstacles or stumbling blocks that will pop up from time-to-time; here's the secret: I gave you that "will power"....I put it on the inside of you

Unless the people in this world are named wisdom and love....and truly personifies those two names....be very careful of the advice that you take from their offerings

You are the Future of Black History, World History and American History; you are the Future History because of your positive mindset, present activities, and your modern-day accomplishments; you are somebody....a very important somebody; you are my sons & my daughters

You are Kings & Queens because you are direct descendants of royalty; you are not chickens... instead you are eagles; eagles are meant to fly high above all others; you have the blood of Kings & Queens in your wings; you have the strength & capacity to overcome anything on earth....you are worthy....you are Kings & Queens; know the strength of your elaborate wings

I pray and prayed everyday for your welfare, safety, love, well-being, strength, honor, integrity, character, etc.; know that there is a blanket of protection around you everyday...because you have a "praying father" via Our Father; my prayers continue along an endless continuum of love...forever and ever more

There is a God....for my eyes have felt him at every turn; continue to seek daily guidance from God; continue to rely on that knowledge & confidence given to you by your earthly father....when needed

You look like God....yes, God is Black; you were created in his image & likeness; stay proud and continue to explore your global History; you are not confined nor defined by this thing or fallacy that we refer to as American History or World History; you are Black....God is Black....stay proud of being Black; this is a huge reason as to why Black is still Beautiful & still Handsome

Don't ever allow anyone....not anyone....to deter you from your truth, your peace, your sanity, nor your dreams

If and when you do fail at something....treat it as a learning exercise; be still and seek the lessons that you can use on your next task or mission

When failure or any negative fallout appears after a project or task.... ask yourself the following questions everytime: 1) what happened, 2) what went wrong, 3) how did it go wrong, 4) how can I prevent it from happening again, 5) apply those lessons forward

When you choose a passion or a career....just make sure that it never becomes a job to you; instead....make sure that your passion is treated in this manner: "I get to" versus "I have to". When your job, career, or passion is a "get to"....you will never work one day in your life; chase your passion & follow your dreams; let your passion & dreams be your "work"

What is Dad's true passion? "You, You, You, You, and You"....because nothing else is more important for me or to me....to accomplish in my life; furthermore, once "You" were born.... "You" gave me purpose & a reason to just enjoy breathing.... thank "You", my children.... thank you so much!!! My passion is You!!!

Understand and know your passion versus your purpose; have a passion & a purpose at every turn

Being a man = having a passion and a purpose

Every morning....look into the mirror and repeat after me: I think like my father, I look like my father, I look like God, I am ready for whatever life throws at me. If you forget to do it every morning.... it's okay....just do it weekly or occasionally (this is an important part of self-affirmation on a daily basis)

Think, do, and then master your subject-matter-of-expertise

Think far beyond your initial thoughts or actions....all while seeking a positive or workable solution

Before you make any large, small....or routine decisions....please take a pause, take 3 deep breaths, and then ask yourself this question: what if? Then, own up to the positive or negative consequences that will follow such a decision

My sons, my daughters, my earthly children, my young men, my young women....I am always with you in deed & spirit; go strong and follow your dreams even stronger....chase happiness strongly....I love you....strongly

Happiness = speak, live, & express your truth....not someone else's truth

Fear is not a word....but more of an acronym; f-e-a-r is false evidence appearing real; don't allow fear to control how high you want to soar; don't allow fear to stop you from enjoying true citizenry....and/or the true essence of you; just remember that I jumped out military planes & fought in the 1990 & 91 Gulf War. If that is not enough....know that I walked this earth as a Man & as a Black Man (fear is not in our vernacular & it should never enter your calculus)

Don't fear....but always know what danger is; know what danger looks like, smells like, etc.; walk or run away from danger....you never need to prove your manhood to anyone; you are a man! Likewise, my daughters....you are a woman!

Know the difference between a disaster versus danger; disaster is something you mop up or clean up, and danger is when you must stop and then get up & avoid it to the best of your ability (try to stay away from or minimize danger); move far from it

Here is why you are special: you are a Child of God, you are my child, and you do not ever have to play second fiddle to anybody on earth; you are first....you are first regardless of the many roles asked of you daily....you are first....forever & always

Live your own-individual and God-given life....not someone else's

You are the greatest....the greatest!!!

3 deep breaths are all you will need to get through any negative situation (police inequalities, evil, racism, terrorism, bad attitudes, parental disagreements, adult mistreatment, different opinions, any debates, any discussions, etc.)....then, think of your own-unique solution; the solution is on the inside of you if you allow your internal light to shine

You are already strong; continue to get stronger with standing up for yourself; every situation is designed to strengthen your stance in life (everybody can get stronger)

Read literature written by Dr. Edwards Robinson pertaining to the Songhai People, the rhapsody, and other writings; appreciate the essence of you & who you truly are (Kings & Queens)

Do you....everyday; stay as positive as you can....but it is very important to let go of a little steam every now & then....but let go of it in a way that maintains your dignity & your respect of self....

Depression, PTSD, insomnia, anxiety, "a little blue", etc....are all real; seek a trusted friend, counselor, or just seek professional help when needed

Don't allow the world (or anybody) to piss on you over & over; it's okay to tell a person these words, "enough....back up....stop....etc.". If that person do not heed your warnings....then move on smartly and try not let that person cross your path

Continue to stand up for justice, equality, and freedom....everyday & everyday....every hour; it's tiring and it's okay to take a mental break from time-to-time

Always tell your truth.... whether your truth "fills" the room or "clears" the room

Don't allow your truth to get you into legal troubles or negative entanglements....and such

Yet....in telling your truth, sometimes you will have to hit the pause button and play a little politics; know when....to say when; follow your guts & instincts in the absence of a clear path to the truth

Truth is truly your only freedom on earth.... truthfully speaking

Political climate nowadays: centered around "good versus evil" instead of "truth versus untruth;" do not take the bait of a political fool and his nonsense....just know & communicate your truth....and stay focused on truth

Don't spend alot of your energies asking "why"....spend most of your energies trying to solve & trying to understand your problems or feelings....or emotions; focus more on lessons that you can learn or use...which can help out on the next situation. Simply put...go deep and find out why you feel a certain way about a certain situation.... and then doctor on those set of emotions

Teach, lead, and continue to lead every chance you get....I made you that way.... "a leader"

Even great leaders need a break every now & then....do not be afraid to have a day which is totally dedicated to self care, self love, self appreciation, etc.

Set aside every Wednesday (or another day)....as your self-care day

Continue to accept advice to advance your thinking beyond being an employee....and focus more on being an employer; business ownership is a huge step toward building generational wealth & building economic freedom

Learn, review, and use the 17 principles that I wrote & published in my first book.... "Simple Poetry, To Whom It May Concern"

You can solve almost every problem in life by knowing the real solution to this simple math problem (without using a calculator).... here is the question or problem: "what is 16% of 50"? Most adults and children would probably start stressing out....and immediately reach for their calculators when asked that question. However, if we relook or rewrite the math problem, we probably would not get so stressed out. For example, without using a calculator, what's 50% of 16? You are right....it is 8. 8 is also the answer to the first math question

The real moral of the aforementioned story: "if we reshape the problems of this society....see the problem for what it is....see & know the root cause of any problem....the solution will be easier to see & know....therefore, it would be easier to solve"

Problem solving = BRASS; BRASS is breathe, relax, aim, stop, steer

No worries about problems....you will encounter tough problems throughout your journey; to use a baseball analogy....your goal should be to never allow your decision to cost you a base; just get to 1st.... you will steal 2nd....then get to 3rd....and you a higher probability to get to home plate

I believe in you

I trust you

I love you

Take 2 minutes everyday to say hallelujah, to say thank you Father and thank you father (dad)...both of these great male figures are constantly saying, "it's our honor to serve you, and you are very welcome"

Every Sunday....after your spiritual hour & other activities....sit still for approximately 10+ minutes to plan out the next 5-7 days & how you plan to accomplish your tasks or missions; create, maintain, & update a personal & work (school) calendar; calendars are your best friends....just don't overcrowd your them (calendars....nor friends); more importantly, don't allow "them" to overcrowd you

Always set or plan time to have some fun.... responsible fun of course

Set a rigid routine everyday and try not to alter it too much (include fun and relaxing things in your daily calendar).

God bless the child who has his or hers own

Don't drive distracted; don't think distracted; don't work distracted; don't study distracted; don't rest distracted; don't sleep distracted; don't fun distracted

What's the main purpose of your calendar beyond the obvious pillars of organization & setting priorities: your calendar is used to tell others "no"

Always look at both sides of the coin before going final with any decision.... regardless of how small or large the decision is at that specific time

Life will "hand you or offer you" solutions or options to every problem; if you have options....you have solutions

Replace any negative mindset of "Dang, I have to do this"....with the mindset of "Wow, I get to do this". By owning the more positive mindset of the day....one is able to see & to appreciate what lies ahead along one's golden journey; your destiny is gold....and I have paved the way for you already....maintain your positive balance & your outlook....you have earned it

This is my finger, this is my hand, there is nothing like "knowing" a Davis' Man; all of my children (men & women) have that Davis' Blood....there is nothing you cannot lead, do, or solve....go get it.... drop the mic

It takes very little to get off that linear path of mental-health fitness; there are alot of peaks, valleys, crooked turns, forks in the road, imbalances, etc.; just handle things one true step at a time; breathe; get adequate-professional support if needed

It's okay to ask for help....on anything.... regardless of how simple or complex of a task...always remember that

Don't try to "make" the decision work; weigh your courses of actions, choose another option, reach another outcome; don't try to force a bad decision to "work out" or to "turnout good"

You belong....in every space, in every organization, in every positive place or space that you want to enter....the space belongs to you....you belong there....you have my blood

You have always been my "hero"; you constantly made me better in every aspect of life

Art of parenting: knowing when to be just a parent....and then knowing when to be a "parent with wisdom"

Parent vs Parent with Wisdom: the difference is that a parent with wisdom knows who, what, where, when, why, and how....in terms of being there for their children. For example, if your child just had a bad day & received an "F" on her report card....the "parent" would probably say immediately, "this is not good, you need to study harder, be quiet in class, organize your notes better, and put in an extra hour of studying per week". Meanwhile, the "Parent with Wisdom" immediately says, "I am so sorry that you have a bad grade on your report card. You have a right to feel terrible & I feel terrible with you. We will come up with a solution". Then, the next day the Wisdom Parent ask the child how can we fix-forward & grab a better outcome the next time. Then, after listening to your child, that Wisdom Parent will probably cover every question known to man. Wisdom knows....proper time & space! The Wisdom Parent knew that his child was already "kicking herself"....and he did not want to kick the child while the child was down. Instead, he gave the child a extra day for introspection....then discussed the important points the next day. Be a Parent with Wisdom!

You do not always have to remain humbled....express your truth; truth is the best form of humility; truth is the greatest form of freedom

Our Father, my father....who art in heaven, are y'all still here? We said and say, "yes"!!!

Since the age of five, you have heard this question....we are going pro in what?....academics! Bachelors, Masters, and Doctorate Degrees

Once you walk through various career doors or entrepreneurship doors, make sure you do not close the door behind you; keep your doors open and bring others along with you....to the best of your abilities

Stay mindful of the fact that there are more evil & ruthless people in the office business world....than on any street in America; watch out for backstabbers because they are constantly smiling in your face; stay alert....stay alive

Find yourself a mentor and friend who will constantly mentor you the right way....a mentor who is unafraid to say, "my door is open.... com'on in".... "my time is your time"

Surround yourself with great friends, great mentors....just great people at all cost

You will constantly be a great friend for & to everyone you meet.... just make sure that you choose one person who you can lean on & share things about your struggles, your depression, your anxieties, your trials, your tribulations, etc.; find that one person who will be a true friend "to you"

Dating advice: you will never be good enough or the right person... for that wrong person in your life; if that person rejects you then that person was the wrong person in your life; try not to internalize rejections; accept the fact that the wrong person was not right for your values & your value system

Marriage advice: don't do it; keep two or three friend girls; let them know where each girl stands; hire a surrogate woman to give birth to your child or children; take complete control & custody of your kids; hire you a nanny to help out with chores & assisting you with parenting activities; enjoy your kids; continue to date two or three different women; enjoy your life to the fullest

If you decide to marry....good luck but these "new females" want to be a man; women are trying to feminize our young men; be careful

Marriage is a bad business investment; she will get half....even if she is ratchet, lazy, unconcerned, & a freak; it's a terrible business investment....just keeping it one hundred

You can love without marriage

Be mindful & careful of those individuals who do not love you; all of them have an angle (good or bad one)....just try to find out his or her angle before it negatively impacts you or your decision

After you read this book....coupled with your past conversations with me....no one will ever be able to "blow smoke up your butt" or BS you....whether it be in your personal life, business, school, church, home, etc.

The only way someone can get over on you is....if you play the role of "fool"....and please hear me on this: everybody plays a fool sometimes....both willingly & unwillingly....and there is no exceptions to this unwritten rule; everybody plays it....or will play it....whether he or she plays it for an hour, a day, a week, or etc. Yet, the final decision is yours in terms of saying, "enough".

Don't cross that creek (keep everything above your high standard); exert high moral & physical courage at all times

Never drink alcohol, never do drugs, never inject anything into your body or bloodstream, only take prescribed or over the counter drugs when necessary....but stay mindful about those meds as well; don't put anything into your body or temple that could damage any portions of your temple

Know what "you" mean to you? I know what you mean to me....but always know what "you" mean to you

Go get a piece of that American P-I-E (performance, image, and exposure); I would ranked these letters in order by putting the letter "I" first.... followed closely by the letter "E"....then the letter "P" would be third (I, E, P)

Image is the most important of the three...followed closely by exposure...and then performance

Networking is akin to exposure; more specifically...networking is all about using your greatest leadership qualities to motivate the opposite person to tell you, "yes"...

As you continue to accomplish your strategic milestones, don't spend alot of time patting yourself on the back....because those people who look up to you & those who know you....will do it (patting) for you

While the world is patting you on the back...say thank you...and keep your eyes on your prize...the next prize...and prizes

Don't forget to take a breather and truly appreciate your accomplishments and accolades...just don't get stuck there

God is Good...all the time...and all the time...God is Good; if this is true...what's the problem...what can man, woman, or any person do to you; success is in you, of you, by you, & for you; just ensure that you use your own definition of success

Continue to speak up & out...in an effort to truly master the English Language; up & out is all about where your skills meets opportunity and you are forced to balance your emotions to obtain truth or a great solution; yet..sometimes you just have to go there & just speak truth to power; you determine when to say when

If you speak well, you will write well; if you write well, you will always be able to express your true ideas, feelings, etc.

When presenting information or data: 1) tell the audience what you plan on telling them, 2) then proceed to tell them, and finally.... 3) summarize everything that you told them. Never forget that you should be brilliant, be brief, and be gone

An essay can also follow the same aforementioned logic too. For example, in your introductory paragraph, your basic language takes on your energy & enthusiasm of saying hello to your audience. Your spirit should be saying, "hello my wonderful audience....here is what I plan to talk or communicate to you about today" (this spirit is generally captured in a topic sentence). Then, in as much simplicity as possible, highlight the three subcategories that you will expound upon as well. Then, immediately within the next three paragraphs.... start expounding upon the three categories....in as much detail as possible. Finally, summarize everything that you just said in the 4 aforementioned paragraphs. Writing is never complicated....just look at it differently....the glass is always half-full

Know what “right” looks like; continue to do the “right” thing.... not just what looks good or feels good

Don’t stop resting your “goods” until your “goods” have climbed the 3-step ladder of good, better, and then best

For example....your baccalaureate degree is good....your masters degree is better....and your doctoral degree is best

You are the captain of your airplane; determine your highest altitude & aptitude....

No matter the assignment, project, mission, or task....run it through the model of good, better, best

School or work: try to avoid cramming....because cramming could lead to high stress; plan and organize your thoughts, tasks, & actions.... then do a little everyday to avoid major pitfalls; sometimes one has to use cramming....but try to avoid this technique as much as possible; setup, use & manage your calendar

Trust your intestinal fortitude (guts)

Never be afraid of introducing yourself to any person, any group, anyone at all....or the world at large....because the world has been awaiting your arrival (you are the greatest)

Any time you say the word, "Dad", I will speak to you and give you guidance through that inner voice within you; that inner voice that you hear....it's me

You do not have to play "hide & seek" to find out who you are and what you love....simply put: I am you....and you are me....you are the greatest!!!

When faced with life's challenges or problems....ask yourself this question: what would Dad do? Listen to your inner spirit for which I speaketh....problem solved.

Your voice is my voice; your choice is my choice

Because you have that Davis' blood....life cannot ever present you with a "problem"....only "challenges"....never problems

I have already given you the solution to all challenges that will masquerade as problems....just continue to trust "your" judgement and your ability to solve anything. You can do all things....and you will....

Look up every morning and say a prayer....there you will find me.... lying comfortably within your elegant grace and constantly saying.... "you got this day....I understand the struggle, the struggle is real.... keep-on keeping on, go-get-em"

While doctoring on your physical and spiritual health....don't forget about your raw emotions, outbursts, and all aspects of your mental health; all are equally important

We change the oil in our vehicles more often than we "check on" our mental health

It's okay....to not be okay....but you cannot heal what you do not reveal; reveal it to yourself and then to a trusted person or professional; seek professional health from a psychiatrist if needed.... especially when anxiety becomes worst. Again, it's okay to not be okay....just seek a healing solution that works best for you and your mental health

Mental health solutions: what works best for you....may not work best for the next person....and vice versa

It's okay "not" to smile every single second of the day....it's okay not to laugh, not to show happiness, or not to show joy every single second of the day. It's okay to tell a person, "I'm not okay", "I'm not feeling my best today," and then seek further help from a trusted person or from a psychiatrist. It's okay....it's okay.

None of this makes you "lesser"....you are not less than a man or less than a woman....it makes you "greater" just to recognize your own discomforts! Now....seek the appropriate help if needed

Be careful and watchful of those people inside your circle or external of it....who will take my quotes and use it for their own benefit or fame....these quotes are "of you, for you, by you and from me"....and intended just for you

Family is not confined by bloodlines....family is only defined by who loves you, who cares for you, who supports you....and the ones who do those things all of the time; you determine who family is & who family should be going forward; I have been extremely lucky & blessed to have my bloodlines as my family....some people are not that lucky or blessed

I think....ergo, therefore, I lived; I love....ergo, therefore, you will continue to live & you will continue to love too

I am here.... because you are still here; if you and I want to live forever....just continue to multiply.... in a responsible way of course; I have done that....I am still here....just look at you (it's me)

My Dad use to say, "tell everyone to treat you like you asked or requested them to treat you....treat me like the man who I am; I am a man"

My Mom use to say, "you are important; life is going to hurt alot.... also know that a hard head will make a soft behind"

Since life is going to hurt from time-to-time....trust your instincts and always listen to your inner voice & inner soul; your inner & outer faculties are me

Strength is not measured in how much you can take nor how much you can handle....nor how much turmoil you have walked through; strength is valuing yourself, making better choices, and allowing positive people around you to add to your existing value of self

You will wake up every morning with two guarantees: a chance... and a choice; trust yourself to continue to make good choices....then better choices....and then the best choices

In life, school, business & at play....try your hands at practicing this technique: under promise....and then over deliver

Prepare, study, then over-prepare, then take a deep breath....and then go and perform....(performing music, refereeing, studying academics, accounting, tutoring, teaching, managing, owning a business, praying, enjoying sports or play of any kind, speaking publicly, living life, rearing kids, maintaining special relationships, etc.)

Me: ready! you: ready! me: ready!

you: ready!

I believe in you, I trust you, and I love you....✓✓✓

When your world & thoughts get too heavy, find you a quiet spot and just speak to me or speak to God....we hear you....and we are with you forever....and ever more

Be the best version of you....because other people's lives are already occupied by someone else....just be you....because you are already great enough

Know the difference between "pressure" vs. "just a situation"

Be sure to share or to tell older people that it is not wise to place their expectations on you or to expect you to solve problems the same way they solve problem. Why? Their selfish expectations will only lead them to immediate disappointment....they will be disappointed while you are moving on with your life. What's the key? To give you the space to enjoy your life, to be creative, and to solve your problems in your own unique way (when, where, and how you want too); trust is ultimate key....and selfish people do not trust others

When & if you lose a competitive event or situation....do three things: do not lose confidence, do not lose the valuable lessons learned from the invaluable experience, and lastly, smile....embrace the lessons & smartly move on to the next best thing

Watch out world....here comes my sons....here comes my daughters

Don't live someone's virtual or social media life....just enjoy your unique life

Create generational wealth through your own initiative and in your own way (rental properties, consulting, tutoring, teaching ACT & SAT workshops, mentoring, collegiate teaching, conducting master classes via interactive videos, conducting private lessons, etc.); entrepreneurship is inside of you

Stay away from as much financial debt as possible; make your first home an apartment....and purchase a rental home to produce rental income and allow your renters to pay your apartment rent (primary residence); only build your own home from the ground up & out of your own pockets; purchase more rental homes to produce more rental income....to allow those particular renters to pay your mortgage on the home that you just built (see the Davis' Business Clock); seek the guidance of a great tax attorney & tax accountant, make your monies work for you....not the other way around

The best way to handle a fight or a huge disagreement: walk the opposite way; allow fools to stay foolish....your Dad did not create a fool....ergo, therefore....you are not a fool

One of our goals when trouble or danger appears: make it home

You are bright, smart, handsome, intelligent, great, full of greatness, a peacemaker, disciplined, structured, thoughtful, kind, inviting, mentally tough, physically tough, spiritually sound, ethically astute, and many upon many of other positive attributes....

I see you! While the wicked world pretends not to see you....I see you!

I respect you....I respect your struggle...I see you!

Without putting yourself in harm's way, help other folks who are truly in need; one of the best gifts that you can give to anybody is a sense of hope, belonging, and an overall helping hand. I spent my life honoring & doing just that. For example, Redd was one of my favorite homeless veterans who I tried to encourage at every turn (for 15+ years....prior to his passing). Yet, all of the veterans that I have helped....are my favorites too; find a charitable cause that speak to your conscience

It's not your job to fix racism because you did not create it; your job is to help any sensible soul to understand that it is wrong and to share your solutions when encountering problems or challenges; never be afraid to share your truth regarding any topic; request that people treat you the way you request to be treated

There is only one true freedom within the belly of this wicked world....and that freedom is "speaking your truth".... everything has been tampered with or tightly monitored (most of the times.... things are monitored illegally, unethically, biasedly, or unfairly).

There is always more work to do....in terms of confronting & challenging racism....and challenging the wicked laws & policies of this land & world; more specifically, there is only smart work to do; light (ness) will prevail over dark (ness); seek and know to the light

The real light = God & truth; heavenly truth & earthly truth

Find something that will keep you moving and staying in shape (physically, emotionally, & mentally)

You cannot do everything at once; prioritize your calendar daily and complete those things that are essentially essential; also continue to practice the word, "no thank you" because it will give you a lot of quality time to & for yourself

"Make time" only for your kids, parents, or children....everybody else should be placed on a calendar

Yet....to be very honest.... sometimes you may even have to place your parents & siblings on a calendar too (dahaha)

Remember to put on your oxygen mask before you try to help others put on their oxygen masks. Why? Because it's hard to help others if you run out of oxygen

Do not beg friends, strangers, or others to like you....do not buy friendship or love....because you are perfectly fine just the way you are; plus those aforementioned type of people do not deserve you & they do not deserve the beauty of your offerings

Bad or inclement weather is God's way of getting us to become still and reflective; do not be afraid of bad weather....just calm your thoughts and say, "thank you, God, for this weather"

Stay alert....stay alive (driving, walking, running, chilling, dating, etc.)

Don't allow friends, colleagues, neighbors, certain family members, etc....to waste your time....because your time is one of your most valuable assets

Time = presence + passion + dreams + commitment + energy

When people rob you of your time, they are trying to steal your presence, passion, dreams, commitment & energy

What is your favorite text message that I have sent you? Write it here in this blank below and share it with a family member or a close friend, or anyone who you choose to share it with....

Marriage & having children: children are a blessing....explore other avenues to marriage....look at having children through a surrogate parent or partner....

Career: chase your passion and you will never work one day in your life; the military was my career passion; my kids are & were my truest passion

Business ownership & wealth building: while chasing your passion.... also build up your business ownership portfolio....think in terms rental income, consulting, mentoring, tutoring, etc.; see detailed email titled, "career"

Music: chase your dreams in music; chase your dreams in sports management; chase your dreams in accounting; become a subject matter expert via obtaining your Doctorate Degree & owning a business venture

Choose a business, job, profession, or passion with this as the main purpose: if I did not have to be concerned with a paycheck....this is what I would do

Retirement: retire by the age of 55 and turn your attention to a second passion....for fun & excitement

Post retirement: monitor & work your private businesses....and enjoy your free time

Tap into your rich history & your rich spirit of your ancestors.... to remember that we are "overcomers" regardless of the world's negative ways or racist views of us

If at first we don't succeed....do the following: dust yourself off, pray, ask for additional guidance, plan for a positive outcome, change the plan accordingly, develop an alternate solution via two possible courses of actions, execute the chosen course of action, rinse, and repeat the process; problems within the world cannot break you or keep you down for too long

Banks only lend monies to create monies; if you want to be rich or wealthy (there is a difference)....then only borrow monies to purchase assets; poor people borrow monies (if they can) and buy only liabilities (hunting equipment, cars, big trucks, motorcycles, overpriced houses, jewelry, various trending items, etc.)

Rich vs wealthy: a rich person has enough monies for himself and maybe his immediate family; a wealthy person never spends his own monies and passes his monies down three, four, five generations.... and then some (generational-wealth building at its finest)

Own rental income properties and pass it down to your kids...and further down the family tree

My dad would always say failure only comes when you try your hardest; find something in life to fail at....but instead of focusing on failure as being the ultimate disappointment....use those failures as teaching points to tell yourself what to do differently the next time you encounter that same situation....or a similar challenge

Know the difference between a gun vs a weapon; a gun is for fighting and a weapon is for protecting your family & yourself; never use a gun but always know how to use a weapon for defense; both could look the same but....entirely different

Don't over sell yourself to world....you are already great & more than great enough

If you had to choose what animal closely resembles you....what would say? My answer would be an eagle. Why? Because an eagle never has to look around and wonder if another animal is flying as high as him. Be an eagle....in all that you do....

Love yourself and never stop loving yourself....no matter of the difficult times that may cross your path....love yourself....because you are worth it....you are the pure essence of love & what love should be

Don't work hard....just work smarter....work smartly; train to standard & not to time

If it does not make monies....it does not make sense or cents; do not give away your services, time, effort, greatness, or smartness for free

You are right....money is not the most important thing in life....but I place it right behind God, My Children (along with the rest of my family), & Oxygen

Irrespective of how many times you fail or lose a competition....never lose "your confidence"....never lose confidence in you

How to maintain confidence? pray, put in more smart work, train to a higher standard, trust your training, breathe, relax, sleep well, rinse, & repeat

There is no secret formula to greatness....(use the formula, on previous page, surrounding "how to maintain confidence")

Conduct a “lockdown weekend” whenever you have something extremely critical to accomplish; tell other people no; it works

In God we trust.... everyone else must sign....sign the paperwork; don’t trust anybody....watch your back at all times; other people’s words are not always their bond

Stay hongry....not hungry....but hongry!!

Don't fear nothing or nobody....but always know danger.....always be able to detect danger; always walk away from danger

The sun can never be fully appreciated without experiencing inclement weather from time-to-time

Therefore, when life issues you problem after problem....just know there is no true progress without true struggle; you were built to solve problems

The sun will shine again....joy, happiness are ours....right now....and in the morning

Arrive super early....everywhere you go; tardiness is for the mass of lazy folks....you are not lazy or nonchalant

A couple of my favorite songs are "Get Down On It", "Harry-Hippie", and "What's Going On". Some of my favorite Spiritual Songs are "Lift Every Voice and Sing", "This Little Light of Mine", "On This Battlefield", and "We Are Soldiers"....just to name a few

My favorite color is Black

Some of my favorite action words are equity, inclusion, freedom, justice, and love; these words always put a fire in my belly

What are a few of my favorite places visited in my early years?

Sontag, Africa, Puerto Rico, Brazil, Hawaii, Nevada, Korea, and Egypt

God bless the world and all the people within its belly. What is my vision of this world....not just America? To become one people who can finally live up to the promises & true intentions of our Creator. Additionally, every person shall be equal, free, treated the same, and loved. How do the world get to this point? By sacrificing their evil ways; eradicating racism (of all kinds) at every turn; truly living in a Godly way behind closed doors; changing evil institutional policies at every level of living or working, treating others like they request to be treated. Yet, none of these things are possible.... without some concrete bases of truth

Integrity is what you do when others are watching you; character is what you do behind closed doors when nobody is looking

Win or lose....just be in the "room" or at the "table"....that's the real reward....being in the room

Once inside the room....know that you have worked like hell to get there....ergo....you belong; you belong everywhere you enter

Males should always choose to be a man of great character; females should always choose to be a woman of great character

Character starts & ends with truth; it never relies on make-believe, fake principles, or any dishonesty of any kind; character = truth

On behalf of your parent and/or parents....I apologize. For what? Anything (large or small) that we did not do right....from start to finish; greatness has flaws too; we did alot of things well but I know you can also tell us what we did wrong too; I apologize and ask for your individual & collective forgiveness....

If White people want to know what if feels like when Black people drive vehicles or when "driving Black" or "just being Black". Just look at any judicial proceedings of any courtroom, any house or congressional hearings, school detentions, lack of diversity & inclusion at your work area or office, etc. All those biases & inequalities....that is what driving black feels like

If a person can pick out one of my quotes that he or she likes or loves...then he or she....more than likely....love the majority of these written quotes too; they are just too ashamed, bashful, or untruthful to admit it; be careful listening to such haters....regardless of his or her title

Supercalifragilisticexpialidocious

my definition and meaning of this word encompasses the following spirit: you can use your imagination and skills to do & to be anyone who you want to be; you are great; you are wise; your life is awaiting you; live your life but do not attempt to live another person's life; create your own smart fantasy & turn it into your own reality; you are the man or the woman; you are my sons & daughters who can accomplish anything under our sun. Life is your sun, your playground, and your masterpiece....so let your light continue to shine as bright as you want it to shine!

My sister use to say to my Mom, "everything will be alright". So, to borrow my sister's thoughts....you, my kids, are way passed alright....you will have your challenges & moments of sadness....but "everything will be alright"

Life is for the living....live "your" life

If life is for the living....then death is for the dying; you are not dead.... so live!!!

Go-get-em....rrrrroooofffff!!!

Again....and it's definitely worth repeating....you (my children) are my hero!

I leave unto you these important gifts: gift of love, gift of character, gift of leadership, gift of true freedom, and the gift of laughter

I love you....my son & my sons!

I love you....my daughter & my daughters!

I love you...my parents, grandparents, & siblings!

I love you....my nieces & nephews (who are my children too)

All of my family tree....I love you!

I believe in you, I trust you, and I love you!!!

Milton Keynes UK
Ingram Content Group UK Ltd.
UKHW041920030823
426310UK00013B/214/J

9 798369 402221